I0697883

The 50+ Freedom Formula: Redefining Retirement

A Guide to Building Your Digital Empire from Home

Contents

Bio Author

As a backend developer specializing in Python and boasting a rich background in the financial sector, G. Scott has emerged as a visionary in the realm of digital entrepreneurship. With experience at leading institutions in health insurance and banking, Scott brings a unique blend of technical skills and business acumen to the table, aimed at empowering individuals in their pursuit of digital independence.

After an intensive journey of self-study and research, during his education and beyond, Scott has amassed a wealth of knowledge on digital entrepreneurship. His book, "The 50+ Freedom Formula: Redefining Retirement," is a distillation of this wisdom, aimed at inspiring peers to take the leap into the digital economy. Scott's approach is grounded in realism and caution, a beacon for those navigating the sometimes turbulent waters of online business.

A graduate of WINC Academy, where he excelled at a high level, Scott embodies the principle of lifelong learning. His transition from financial professional to a respected name in music production with Logic Pro X, and now to an AI specialist and programmer, is a testament to an insatiable appetite for knowledge and self-improvement. Scott's story is a powerful example of how it's never too late to embark on new paths, regardless of age.

Outside his professional pursuits, Scott has diverse interests, ranging from art and cooking to fashion and space exploration, making him a well-rounded and deeply engaging individual. His commitment to helping others, both in the community and the animal kingdom, speaks of a deep-rooted empathy and connection to life in all its forms.

With plans to share his insights and success, Scott is poised not only to shape his legacy but also to inspire others to embrace their potential, regardless of their stage in life. His story is not just a testament to what's possible in the digital age but also an invitation to join in this exciting journey.

Who Is This Book For?

Empowering Your Digital Entrepreneurship Journey After 50

Welcome to "The 50+ Freedom Formula: Redefining Retirement," a comprehensive guide designed for individuals over 50 eager to embrace digital entrepreneurship and secure their financial independence. Whether you're contemplating a new career direction, enhancing your retirement, or looking to transform your golden years into a time of growth and opportunity, this book is your strategic companion.

Tailored Insights for the Aspiring 50+ Entrepreneur:

Our guide is specifically crafted for those who may not have a deep background in digital technology but possess the desire and drive to venture into this promising domain. We distill complex concepts into actionable steps, providing a clear path through the digital business landscape.

What You Will Gain:

- Foundational Knowledge: Access a wealth of information that spans various digital business models, offering insights into selecting the right path that resonates with your passions and goals.

- Practical Strategies: From conceptualizing your digital product to mastering online marketing, discover a series of step-by-step strategies that demystify the process of launching and growing an online business.

- Inspirational Stories: Draw motivation from real-life success stories of individuals who have triumphed over age stereotypes to build flourishing digital enterprises.

Transforming Vision into Reality:

This book goes beyond mere theory, providing you with a clear framework to actualize your digital entrepreneurship ambitions. Whether your aim is to craft a passive income source or actively manage a burgeoning online business, "The 50+ Freedom Formula" equips you with the knowledge, tools, and confidence to turn your vision into a successful digital reality.

Embark on Your Digital Journey:

It's time to redefine retirement and turn your later years into a vibrant, productive, and financially rewarding era. Join us as we navigate the exciting world of digital entrepreneurship together, crafting a future that's not only secure but also aligned with your passions and aspirations.

Introduction:

Embracing a New Chapter

The Contemporary Retirement Challenge

The concept of retirement is undergoing a radical transformation. Gone are the days when retirement meant a guaranteed pension and a future of leisure. Today, for those over 50, the landscape is shifting—traditional retirement savings are no longer a surefire plan due to an evolving job market, insufficient pensions, and the increasing cost of living. This book delves into these challenges, offering a fresh perspective on what retirement can and should look like.

The Promise of Digital Entrepreneurship

Amidst these challenges lies an extraordinary opportunity: the realm of digital entrepreneurship. This venture is more than just a financial safety net; it's a pathway to personal satisfaction and independence. We simplify the digital domain, illustrating how it's a fertile ground for the 50+ demographic to innovate and prosper, transforming their wisdom and passions into thriving online ventures.

What Sets This Book Apart

This guide is unique in its celebration of the mature generation's accumulated wisdom, viewing it as an invaluable asset in the digital marketplace. We combine inspiring success stories, actionable advice, and an in-depth exploration of digital entrepreneurship to equip you with the tools to apply your life's learnings to achieve online success.

Your Journey to Digital Entrepreneurship

We'll walk you through the fundamental steps of launching and expanding an online business, offering a detailed roadmap and motivational insights. Whether it's identifying lucrative niches or excelling in digital marketing, this book marks the beginning of your transformative journey. Here, retirement is reimagined—not as the final chapter but as a vibrant new beginning filled with potential for growth, innovation, and financial independence.

1

The First Step Towards Your Digital Empire

Embracing Change: Strategies to Overcome Age-Related Biases and the Fear of Technology

Welcome to the starting line of a journey that promises not just a new career path, but a vibrant, exciting future. This isn't just a step; it's a giant leap into the world of digital entrepreneurship — a place where the only limits are the boundaries of your imagination. Whether you're looking to reinvent yourself after decades in a traditional job, or simply eager to add more zest to your later years, this book is your compass, your map, and your friendly guide all rolled into one.

As we dive into the digital domain, we're confronted with a landscape that's buzzing with opportunity. Yes, it can feel like a maze, with twists and turns that seem daunting at first glance. But within these pages lies the secret to navigating this maze with the grace of a seasoned explorer. You're not just trying to keep up; you're here to lead the way, to carve out a niche that's uniquely yours, and to claim a piece of the digital frontier that awaits your mark.

This chapter lays the groundwork for a thrilling expedition. It's dedicated to tearing down those walls of doubt — the age-related myths that say 'it's too late,' and the fears of technology that whisper 'it's too complicated.' Here, you'll find practical strategies and real talk that will not only boost your confidence but also arm you with the knowledge to embrace change with open arms.

We're going to demystify the digital world, showing you that it's not a playground reserved for the young tech-savvy alone. It's a vast expanse where experience is valued, where wisdom is a currency, and where your lifetime of learning and working is a competitive advantage waiting to be leveraged.

Get ready to be inspired by stories of folks just like you who have made their mark and redefined what it means to be a 'retiree.' With each page, you'll feel more prepared, more excited, and more driven to take that bold leap. This isn't just about building a business; it's about building a life that's rich with purpose and brimming with possibilities.

So turn the page, and let's get started. Your digital empire isn't going to build itself, but by the time you're done with this book, you'll have everything you need to begin constructing it, one click at a time.

Understanding the Landscape

Embarking on this digital journey, let's zoom in on the landscape ahead. The digital world is vast and varied, and for those over 50, it presents a unique set of challenges and opportunities. While the pace of technological advancement is rapid, it also opens doors to new ways of thinking, earning, and connecting.

The landscape is not just about the tools and technologies; it's about understanding the ecosystem - the market trends, the online communities, and the ever-evolving consumer behaviors. It's a realm where your accumulated wisdom is not just valuable; it's a competitive edge. Your ability to adapt, to learn, and to apply your life experiences to digital scenarios is what will set you apart.

In this digital terrain, staying informed and agile is key. It's about identifying the digital trends that align with your interests and leveraging them to your advantage. The digital world is not a monolith; it's a mosaic of opportunities waiting to be explored and harnessed.

As we delve deeper into "Strategies for Embracing Change," we'll navigate this landscape with precision, identifying the tools and tactics that will empower you to thrive. We're not just traversing this terrain; we're mastering it, using our insights and experiences to carve out a successful path in the digital domain.

Strategies for Embracing Change

1. Challenge Age-Related Biases: It's not just important, it's essential to stand up to the old myths about age and tech. Remember, the wisdom, experience, and the extensive network you've developed over the years? These aren't just bonuses; they're your secret weapons in the digital world. Use them to carve out your unique place in the digital landscape.

2. Cultivate a Growth Mindset: See every day as a chance to learn something new, to get a step closer to tech-savviness. Embrace the idea that with time and effort, you can master any skill, including navigating the digital world. Think of every challenge as a stepping stone, not a stumbling block, transforming obstacles into opportunities for growth.

3. Leverage Community and Support Networks: Dive into the wealth of knowledge and camaraderie available in online communities and forums dedicated to digital entrepreneurship. Here, you're not alone; you're part of a collective journey, with access to insights, advice, and encouragement specifically tailored to your path.

4. Demystify Technology: Start with the basics and steadily build your tech prowess. Utilize platforms like Coursera, Udemy, and Khan Academy, where you can find a plethora of courses — many free or at a minimal cost — that offer practical, hands-on skills in tune with your entrepreneurial ambitions.

5. Celebrate Small Wins: Every step forward, no matter how minor it seems, is a victory in your journey to digital mastery and entrepreneurial success. These moments of triumph are the building blocks of your confidence and momentum. So, give yourself a pat on the back for every hurdle crossed and every new skill acquired.

Real-Life Inspiration

Meet Linda Thompson, who at 60, transformed her love for weaving tales into a thriving digital presence. As a former educator, Linda wasn't initially tech-savvy, but her desire to share her stories was stronger than any hurdle. She started small, with just one blog, learning and growing one click at a time. Her journey wasn't just about writing; it was about connecting. By diving into social media marketing, Linda didn't just find an audience; she built a community, turning her passion for storytelling into a series of workshops that now inspire others across the globe.

Then there's Rajiv Mehta, 55, who brought a fresh breath to retail with his commitment to the planet. With a rich background in retail, Rajiv saw an opportunity where others saw waste. He launched an e-commerce platform dedicated to sustainable home goods, combining his retail acumen with a passion for eco-friendly products. His journey is a testament to how understanding your niche and staying true to your values can pave the way to success in the digital marketplace.

Don't forget Monica Rivera, 52, whose hobby of crafting handmade jewelry became her digital success story. Monica's initial venture into the online world was filled with trepidation, but her determination to share her art drove her forward. She immersed herself in digital marketing courses and community forums, gradually

demystifying the digital world. Now, her Instagram isn't just a showcase of her creations; it's a magnet for jewelry lovers everywhere, turning her passion into a prosperous online business.

Conclusion

Embarking on the path of digital entrepreneurship is an exhilarating step, particularly as you confront and overcome age-related biases and any initial trepidation about technology. This chapter sets the foundation for what's to come, empowering you to transform potential obstacles into opportunities for growth and innovation in your digital empire.

By embracing a proactive learning mindset, valuing the unique strengths and experience you bring, and connecting with supportive online communities, you're not just starting a journey—you're pioneering your path in the digital world. Remember, the realm of digital entrepreneurship isn't reserved for the young but is ripe with opportunities for the young at heart—those who are eager to grasp the new possibilities that await, regardless of age.

The narratives of Linda, Rajiv, and Monica serve as beacons of what's achievable with the right mindset and resources, illustrating that significant digital accomplishments are not only possible but expected. As we delve deeper into this book, let these stories inspire you to craft your own success narrative in the expansive digital landscape.

This is just the beginning. With each chapter, you'll gain more insights and tools to build and scale your digital presence. Embrace the journey ahead with curiosity, courage, and the readiness to transform your later years into a period of growth, innovation, and success in the digital domain.

Goal Setting for Success: Applying SMART Goals and OKRs in Digital Entrepreneurship for the 50+

Setting sail on the digital entrepreneurship sea after 50 isn't just about chasing dreams; it's about charting a course with precision and clarity. This part of your journey is where dreams get transformed into actionable plans, where your aspirations get grounded in reality. We'll dive into the art of setting SMART goals and implementing Objectives and Key Results (OKRs), essential tools that offer a compass and a map for your digital voyage.

As you steer your ship into the digital entrepreneurship waters post-50, it's crucial to have more than just a destination in mind; you need a navigational plan. SMART goals and OKRs are your sextant and stars in this endeavor, guiding you with precision towards your entrepreneurial horizon.

SMART goals ensure your objectives are Specific, Measurable, Achievable, Relevant, and Time-bound, turning the nebulous into the tangible. They're about making your dreams dissectible into bite-sized, manageable tasks that you can tackle systematically.

On the other hand, OKRs push you further, asking you to outline ambitious Objectives and track your progress with quantifiable Key Results. It's about setting your sights high and then breaking down that vision into measurable steps that will march you towards success.

This section will not only explain these concepts but will also show you how to weave them into the fabric of your digital entrepreneurship journey. By the end, you'll have a clear blueprint for turning your post-50 years into a period of achievement, growth, and digital innovation.

The Importance of Goal Setting in Digital Entrepreneurship

Goal setting is a cornerstone of success for any entrepreneur, especially crucial when embarking on a new digital venture. It's about crafting a roadmap for your journey, ensuring each step is intentional and aligned with your ultimate destination. This process isn't just about identifying what you want to achieve; it's about embedding your goals with deep-seated purpose and clarity, ensuring they resonate with your personal and professional aspirations.

Navigating with **SMART** Goals

The SMART framework acts as your compass in the vast ocean of entrepreneurship, guiding you to set goals that are not just wishes but actionable targets:

1. Specific: Clarity is your ally. Instead of a nebulous aim like "I want to start a blog," pinpoint your ambition: "I will launch a gardening blog targeting urban dwellers."

2. Measurable: Quantify your success. Don't just aspire to attract subscribers; set a concrete milestone: "Reach 1000 subscribers in six months."

3. Achievable: Ensure your goals are within reach, given your resources and constraints.

4. Relevant: Your goals should resonate with your larger business ethos and personal principles.

5. Time-bound: Set deadlines to infuse your journey with a sense of urgency and purpose, such as "launch the blog within three months."

Elevating Goals with **OKRs**

While SMART goals lay the groundwork, Objectives and Key Results (OKRs) elevate your ambition. They pair lofty objectives with tangible outcomes, fostering a culture of achievement and accountability:

- **Objective:** State your aim boldly and inspiringly, like "To become the go-to online resource for urban gardening."

- **Key Results:** Attach specific, measurable outcomes to track your progress, such as "Publish 50 in-depth gardening guides" or "Increase website traffic by 40%."

By intertwining SMART goals with OKRs, you not only set a direction for your digital enterprise but also create a dynamic framework to track, measure, and celebrate your progress as you transform your digital aspirations into reality.

Implementing SMART Goals and OKRs in Your Strategy

Kickstart your journey by penning down the dreams you have for your digital business. What begins as broad aspirations will soon take the form of structured, actionable SMART goals. This transformation is about clarity and commitment, turning 'someday' into 'scheduled.'

Once your SMART goals are in place, it's time to level up your strategy with OKRs. This powerful framework takes your goals a step further, integrating them into every facet of your digital venture. Whether it's content creation, marketing prowess, or fostering a vibrant community, OKRs help you set clear objectives and measurable results that align with your overarching mission.

1. From Aspirations to Action: List out what you envision for your digital business. It could be anything from launching a new service to growing your online presence.

2. Crafting SMART Goals: Refine your list into well-defined SMART goals. For each goal, ask how it meets the Specific, Measurable, Achievable, Relevant, and Time-bound criteria.

3. Elevating with OKRs: For every critical area of your business, like content creation, set an Objective that's ambitious yet inspiring. Then, break it down into Key Results that are concrete and measurable.

By systematically implementing SMART goals and OKRs, you're not just planning for success; you're building a scaffold that supports and guides your growth in the digital space, ensuring every step you take is purposeful and impactful.

Real-Life Application: Transforming Passions into Digital Successes

Robert Kim's (61) journey from a marketing executive to an online photography instructor is a testament to the power of strategic goal setting. With a clear vision to share his photography expertise, Robert employed SMART goals to delineate his objectives precisely. He didn't stop there; through OKRs, he aimed to enroll 500 students within the year and foster a community where budding photographers could thrive. This meticulous planning allowed him not just to reach but surpass his targets, adjusting his strategies along the way to capture success beyond his initial aspirations.

Maria Chen (53) transitioned from IT to becoming a beacon for seniors navigating technology. By establishing SMART goals, Maria set a concrete timeline for her tech blog's launch, ensuring each step was purposeful and measured. Her OKRs went further, setting sights on engaging 10,000 monthly visitors and creating content that wasn't just informative but interactive. The result? A blog that resonates with and empowers its audience, turning passive readers into active participants in the tech world.

Jamal Ahmed's (49) culinary journey took a digital turn when he applied SMART goals and OKRs to evolve his catering business into an online culinary classroom. His goals weren't just about broadening his audience but deepening the experience, aiming for a 300% increase in class sign-ups and establishing collaborations with culinary schools. This approach not only broadened his brand's horizons but also seasoned his platform with diverse culinary insights, enriching the learning experience for his students.

These stories underscore how SMART goals and OKRs can transform passions and expertise into flourishing digital ventures, providing a structured path to follow and milestones to celebrate along the entrepreneurial journey.

Conclusion

Embracing digital entrepreneurship after 50 is an exciting venture, and utilizing SMART goals and OKRs is your blueprint for success. These strategies do more than just map out your journey; they turn your vision into achievable, meaningful milestones that resonate with your entrepreneurial aspirations. The power of goal setting is in its dual nature—meticulous in planning and flexible in execution, allowing you to adapt and refine your objectives as you delve deeper into the digital landscape.

By setting SMART goals, you create a foundation built on specifics and measurable outcomes, ensuring each step you take is deliberate and purposeful. Integrating OKRs elevates this process, connecting ambitious objectives with measurable results, and keeping your eyes on the prize while staying grounded in reality.

As you embark on this exciting path, remember that goal setting is not a one-time task but a continuous cycle of setting, achieving, and revisiting your objectives. It's this dynamic approach that will guide you through the evolving world of digital entrepreneurship, helping you to not only reach but exceed your aspirations.

Finding Your Digital Niche: Techniques to Identify Opportunities That Align with Your Experiences and Interests

Venturing into the digital world offers a landscape brimming with opportunities, but the key to making a mark lies in discovering your own niche—a special corner of the market that you can call your own. This isn't just about choosing a focus area; it's about identifying a space where your personal interests, professional skills, and the market's needs intersect in perfect harmony.

In this section, we'll guide you through a series of techniques designed to help you pinpoint your niche, ensuring it's a reflection of what you love, what you're good at, and what the world needs. Whether you're a seasoned professional or newly exploring the digital domain, finding your niche is your first step toward building a meaningful and successful online presence.

1. Reflect on Your Passions and Skills

Kickstart your niche-finding mission by listing down what excites you and where your skills lie. Maybe you're an avid gardener with a knack for teaching, or perhaps coding is your forte. It's where your personal joys meet your professional prowess that the magic happens, guiding you toward a niche that's not only profitable but also fulfilling.

2. Research Market Demand

Now, it's time to play detective in the digital world. Use tools like Google Trends to understand what's catching fire in the realms you're passionate about. Dive into online communities—Reddit threads, LinkedIn groups, or Twitter chats—to get a pulse on what people are talking about, what they need, and what's currently underserved.

3. Identify Problems You Can Solve

Every successful digital niche solves a problem or fills a gap. Examine your areas of interest through a problem-solving lens. Maybe your potential customers are crying out for easy-to-understand tech tutorials, or perhaps there's a shortage of quality online cooking classes focusing on dietary restrictions. If you can pinpoint a problem and address it uniquely, you've struck niche gold.

4. Analyze the Competition

Understanding who you're up against can offer strategic insights. What are they doing well? Where are they falling short? This isn't about copying—it's about finding your edge. Maybe you can offer more personalized service, deeper expertise, or a fresh perspective that's currently lacking in the market.

5. Validate Your Niche

Before diving in, test the waters. Share some blog posts, videos, or social media content in your prospective niche. The feedback and engagement you receive will be invaluable. It's not just about confirming interest—it's about refining your approach based on real-world reactions.

6. Start Small and Iterate

Launch with a focused, laser-sharp vision but remain agile. The digital world is dynamic, and feedback is immediate. Use it to fine-tune and evolve your niche, ensuring that it continues to resonate with your audience and stays ahead of market trends.

By methodically working through these steps, you'll not only discover a niche that's the perfect fit for you but also lay the groundwork for a venture that's both personally rewarding and market-relevant.

Conclusion

Pinpointing your digital niche is more than just the first step—it's the cornerstone of creating a digital venture that not only brings financial rewards but also personal satisfaction. When your niche is a reflection of your passions and skills and meets a clear market demand, you're not just setting up a business; you're crafting a venture that's uniquely yours, poised for long-term success in the digital landscape.

However, remember, the journey doesn't conclude with the discovery of your niche. The digital world is ever-changing, and so are the needs and interests of your audience. To thrive, not just survive, it's crucial to continuously evolve within your niche, adapting and growing in response to new trends and feedback. This dynamic approach ensures your digital enterprise remains relevant, engaging, and at the forefront of your industry.

Digital Business 101: A Beginner's Guide to Starting an Online Business

Embarking on the journey of digital entrepreneurship is an exciting venture that requires a solid grasp of the basics of online business. This guide is designed to demystify the process, providing you with a clear, step-by-step framework to get your digital business off the ground. From selecting the right business model to crafting your online identity, we've got you covered.

1. Choosing Your Business Model

The foundation of your digital venture is your business model. Here are some options to consider:

- **E-commerce:** Sell products online directly to your customers.
- **Affiliate Marketing:** Earn commission by promoting products or services from other businesses.
- **Content Creation:** Launch a blog, a YouTube channel, or a podcast to share your expertise or entertain.

- **Online Consulting or Coaching:** Use your knowledge to offer advice or coaching services online.

Assess how each model aligns with your passions, skills, and lifestyle goals to choose the best fit for you.

2. Setting Up Your Online Presence

Your digital storefront is where customers connect with your brand. Here's how to establish it:

- **Website Builders:** Platforms like WordPress, Wix, or Shopify make it easy to create your own site, even without technical skills.
- **Domain Name and Hosting:** Choose a catchy domain name and a reliable hosting service to ensure your website is fast and always accessible.
- **Design and User Experience:** Your website should be visually appealing and easy to navigate, providing a positive experience on both desktops and mobile devices.

3. Creating Valuable Content

Content is the lifeblood of your digital presence:

- Craft informative, engaging content that showcases your expertise and provides real value to your audience.

- Use SEO strategies to improve your site's visibility on search engines, drawing more visitors to your content.

4. Building Your Audience

Grow your community by connecting with your audience across various digital channels:

- **Social Media:** Engage with your audience on platforms they frequent, sharing content that sparks interaction and drives traffic back to your site.
- **Email Marketing:** Develop a subscriber list to share updates, insights, and exclusive offers directly with your followers.

5. Monetization Strategies

Once you've built a solid audience, explore ways to generate revenue:

- **Direct Sales:** Offer your products or services for sale on your platform.
- **Advertising:** Display ads on your website to earn revenue.
- **Affiliate Marketing:** Recommend third-party products and earn a commission for each sale through your referral.
- **Subscriptions:** Provide premium content or services for a subscription fee.

By following these steps, you'll be well on your way to launching a successful digital business that not only meets your financial goals but also aligns with your personal values and passions.

Creating Valuable Content and Mastering SEO

While crafting engaging and informative content is crucial, making sure it reaches your target audience is equally important. This is where Search Engine Optimization, or SEO, becomes vital. SEO involves a set of practices designed to improve your website's visibility in search engine results, making it easier for people to find you online.

- **Understand Keywords:** Identify and use relevant keywords that your target audience is searching for. These should be integrated naturally into your content, titles, and meta descriptions.
- **Optimize for User Experience:** Search engines favor websites that provide a good user experience, which includes fast loading times, mobile responsiveness, and easy navigation.
- **Create Quality Content:** Consistently produce high-quality, original content that addresses the needs and interests of your audience. Search engines reward content that is valuable to users.
- **Build Backlinks:** Links from other reputable websites to your site can significantly boost your SEO rankings. They signal to search engines that others vouch for your content.
- **Stay Updated:** SEO practices evolve as search engine algorithms change, so it's crucial to stay informed about the latest trends and updates in SEO.

By prioritizing SEO in your digital strategy, you'll not only enhance your online presence but also ensure that your valuable content reaches the right people at the right time,

maximizing your business's potential for growth and
success.

Conclusion

Launching a digital business might seem daunting at first
glance, but by breaking down the journey into manageable
steps, it becomes much less intimidating. Focus on
mastering each stage one by one. It's vital to remember
that every accomplished online entrepreneur started where
you are now - with that first, decisive step.

Your path to digital entrepreneurship should be marked by
dedication, innovation, and an eagerness to learn and
adapt. By committing to these principles, you'll not only
navigate the complexities of building an online business
but also discover immense personal and professional
satisfaction along the way.

Embrace this journey with an open mind and a resilient
spirit. With time, what starts today as a small venture can
blossom into a thriving digital business that aligns with
your passions and meets your financial goals. Keep moving
forward, stay curious, and let your entrepreneurial spirit
shine.

2

Building the Foundations of Your Online Presence

Branding with Purpose: Crafting a Brand That Mirrors Your Values and Engages Your Audience

Creating a brand is more than picking a color palette or designing a logo; it's about establishing an identity that encapsulates the core of what you offer and its value to your audience. For digital entrepreneurs, particularly those leveraging a wealth of life experience, your brand is a reflection of your wisdom, experiences, and the unique perspective you bring to the table. In this section, we'll guide you through identifying your fundamental values, understanding your audience, and effectively communicating your brand's story.

1. Identify Your Core Values

Start with a deep dive into what matters most to you and how these values can be integrated into your business's DNA. Whether it's an unwavering commitment to quality, a passion for sustainability, or a dedication to transparency and education, these values should form the foundation of your brand, influencing everything from the content you create to how you engage with customers.

2. Understand Your Audience

Knowing who you're speaking to is crucial. Utilize tools and strategies such as surveys, social media engagement, and market research to get a clear picture of your target audience's needs, challenges, and aspirations. This insight will enable you to tailor your brand's messaging to resonate deeply with them.

3. Communicate Your Brand

With a solid grasp of your values and audience, it's time to bring your brand to life. Choose visuals that reflect your brand's essence, craft a compelling narrative, and ensure consistency across all digital platforms. Every interaction, from your website to your social media profiles to your email campaigns, should consistently reinforce what your brand stands for.

4. Engage and Grow Your Community

A strong brand not only gains recognition but also earns love and advocacy. Engage with your audience by providing valuable content, responsive interactions, and initiatives that center around community building. Encourage feedback, foster discussions, and create spaces where your audience can connect with you and each other. This engagement will not only enhance your brand's presence but also build a loyal community around it.

Real-Life Example

Consider the story of Julia Henderson, who, at the age of 62, launched a thriving online coaching business following her retirement. Her brand, committed to empowering women over 50 to embrace entrepreneurship, was a direct reflection of her own life story and values. Julia utilized targeted social media campaigns, engaging online workshops, and an active community forum to establish a brand that deeply resonated with her audience. This strategic branding effort not only differentiated her in the market but also built a solid foundation for her business, supported by a dedicated and growing community.

Conclusion

Creating a strong, purpose-driven brand is not just an activity; it's an essential strategy for any digital entrepreneur. It's the foundation upon which your entire online business rests, crucial for distinguishing yourself in a crowded digital landscape. A well-crafted brand that reflects your core values and resonates with your audience's expectations doesn't just help you stand out; it fosters genuine connections with your audience, turning casual visitors into loyal supporters.

By intentionally shaping your brand to embody what you stand for and aligning it with the desires and needs of your target market, you position your business for sustained success. This strategic approach to branding not only elevates your visibility in the digital realm but also builds a lasting legacy, ensuring your digital venture thrives in a continuously evolving marketplace.

Essential Digital Tools: An Overview of Accessible Technologies and Platforms That Simplify Online Business Operations

In the dynamic world of digital entrepreneurship, having the right set of tools can significantly streamline your business processes, enhance productivity, and elevate customer engagement. This section delves into essential digital tools and platforms that are designed to be user-friendly, ensuring even those new to the digital scene can navigate with ease.

1. Website Builders:

Creating a professional-looking website is no longer a domain exclusive to tech experts. Platforms like Wix, Squarespace, and WordPress democratize web design with their user-friendly drag-and-drop interfaces, a variety of templates, and integrated hosting services. These tools empower you to establish a robust online presence, even without a background in web development.

2. Social Media Management Tools:

In today's digital landscape, maintaining an active and strategic social media presence is key to building your brand and connecting with your audience. Tools such as Buffer, Hootsuite, and Later streamline this process, allowing you to schedule posts, track engagement, and manage multiple accounts from a single dashboard, ensuring your social media efforts are both effective and efficient.

3. Email Marketing Software:

Email remains a powerful tool for engaging with your audience, promoting your offerings, and building customer relationships. Platforms like Mailchimp and Constant Contact simplify email marketing with easy-to-use interfaces, automation capabilities, and segmentation options, helping you craft targeted campaigns that resonate with your audience.

4. E-commerce Solutions:

For entrepreneurs in the e-commerce space, platforms like Shopify and WooCommerce offer comprehensive solutions that cover everything from product listings to payment processing. These platforms are designed to be intuitive, removing the complexities of online selling and making it accessible to individuals without technical expertise.

5. Analytics and SEO Tools:

A successful digital business relies on data-driven decisions and visibility. Tools like Google Analytics offer insights into your website's performance and user behavior, while SEO tools such as Yoast SEO provide guidance on optimizing your content for search engines, helping you improve your site's ranking and attract more traffic.

By integrating these essential digital tools into your business operations, you can optimize your workflows, engage with your audience more effectively, and enhance your online presence, setting a solid foundation for your digital venture's success.

Real-Life Application:

Michael Thompson's (65) transition from the educational sector to digital entrepreneurship exemplifies the impactful role of digital tools in establishing and expanding an online business. Upon retiring, Michael launched an online consultancy aimed at educational institutions. By harnessing the power of user-friendly digital tools, he successfully crafted a strong online presence and expanded his reach.

Using Squarespace, Michael developed a professional website without needing to delve into complex coding, showcasing his consultancy services effectively. With Buffer, he streamlined his social media strategy, scheduling posts and engaging with his audience efficiently across multiple platforms. Mailchimp became his go-to for email marketing, enabling him to keep his audience informed and engaged with regular updates and valuable content.

But Michael didn't stop there. Recognizing the importance of data and visibility, he employed Google Analytics to track his website's performance and understand his audience better. Coupled with adhering to SEO best practices, he optimized his online content, improving his site's search engine ranking and drawing more potential clients to his consultancy.

Michael's story is a testament to how leveraging the right digital tools can transform a retiree's expertise into a thriving online business, demonstrating that age is merely a number when it comes to digital entrepreneurship.

Conclusion

Navigating the digital landscape becomes an empowering experience when you leverage the right tools and technologies designed to elevate your entrepreneurial endeavors. Familiarizing yourself with these essential instruments and incorporating them into your strategy can significantly amplify your online presence, streamline your operations, and foster deeper connections with your audience.

These tools are not just facilitators; they're catalysts that can transform your digital aspirations into tangible successes. They offer you the means to efficiently manage your business, engage with your target market, and analyze your progress, ensuring that every decision is data-driven and every strategy is audience-centric.

Whether you're at the threshold of launching a digital venture or in the midst of expanding your online empire, embracing these digital tools is pivotal. They don't just support your business; they propel it forward, setting a solid foundation for your success in the dynamic digital marketplace.

Launching Your First Offering: Deep Dive into Successful Market Entry

Embarking on the journey from ideation to the actual launch of your digital product or service is a momentous milestone in your entrepreneurial path. This section is meticulously crafted to guide you through the critical steps for a triumphant introduction to the market, drawing inspiration from those who've paved the way in the digital arena.

1. Product or Service Development:

The genesis of your offering lies in a well-articulated concept that addresses a specific need or problem. Start with defining what you're offering in explicit terms, highlighting its unique problem-solving capabilities and what sets it apart in the crowded digital space. Market research is indispensable at this stage; utilize platforms like SurveyMonkey or Google Forms to garner insights directly from your target audience, refining your product or service to better meet their needs.

2. Branding and Packaging:

The essence of your offering is significantly influenced by its branding and packaging. These elements should resonate with your intended audience, encapsulating the core message of your product or service. Leverage design tools like Canva and Adobe Spark to create visually appealing and cohesive branding materials that consistently communicate your offering's value proposition across all customer touchpoints.

3. Online Presence:

Your digital footprint is anchored by your online presence, primarily your website or a specific product landing page. This virtual space should be designed with the user in mind, featuring clear calls to action (CTAs), intuitive navigation, and an easy process for users to engage with your offering, whether that's making a purchase or signing up for a service.

4. Marketing Strategy:

A robust marketing strategy is your roadmap to reaching and resonating with your target audience. It should encompass a mix of digital marketing channels tailored to where your audience is most active, including social media, content marketing, email campaigns, and possibly targeted advertisements. Employ analytics tools to track the effectiveness of your campaigns and iterate based on data-driven insights.

5. Launch Preparation:

The anticipation build-up to your launch is crucial. Utilize teaser content, email newsletters, and social media announcements to spark interest and generate buzz. Consider special promotions or early access for your initial followers to create a sense of exclusivity and urgency.

6. Post-Launch Activities:

The launch is just the beginning. Post-debut, focus on gathering and implementing customer feedback to refine your offering continuously. Maintain engagement with your audience through consistent communication and outstanding customer service, laying the foundation for a loyal customer base and facilitating organic growth through referrals and word-of-mouth.

Real-Life Example: The Comprehensive Journey of Emily Robertson

Emily Robertson, after her retirement at 63, didn't see the culmination of her career in education as an endpoint but as a springboard into a new venture—launching "Mindful Moves," an innovative online wellness platform. Her journey underscores not just the strategic deployment of digital tools but the embodiment of resilience and adaptability in the face of entrepreneurship's unpredictable nature.

With a profound understanding of her target audience— busy professionals seeking balance and wellness—Emily embarked on a meticulous market research phase. She wasn't just looking for surface-level data; she sought deep insights into the challenges, preferences, and unmet needs of her potential customers. Utilizing tools like SurveyMonkey, she gathered feedback that would become the cornerstone of her service offerings.

Emily's approach to branding and online presence was anything but conventional. She delved into storytelling, weaving her personal journey and passion for wellness into the brand narrative, making "Mindful Moves" not just a service but a story that her audience could connect with. Her choice of Squarespace as her website platform was strategic, enabling her to craft an online space that reflected the essence of her brand—serene, inviting, and user-centric.

But her journey was more than just setting up the right tools. As the launch day approached, Emily engaged her burgeoning community with more than just teasers and sneak peeks. She initiated conversations, shared valuable tips, and even offered a glimpse into the making of her platform, building a relationship with her audience that went beyond transactional interactions.

Her launch strategy was a blend of personal outreach, leveraging her network, and smart marketing. Email campaigns weren't just announcements; they were invitations to join her in this new chapter, complemented by targeted ads and social media strategies that expanded her reach.

Post-launch, Emily's commitment to her community shone even brighter. She didn't just seek feedback; she engaged in dialogues, making her customers feel heard and valued. Each piece of feedback was a gem, used to refine and enhance her offerings. Her platform wasn't static; it evolved, mirroring the growth and changing needs of her audience.

Emily Robertson's story is a testament to the fact that launching a digital offering in later life is not just about employing the right tools but about embedding your venture with your values, story, and the unwavering belief that it's never too late to start anew.

Conclusion:

The launch of your digital product or service is a thrilling yet challenging endeavor that sets the stage for your business's future. Drawing on the strategies and insights from successful digital entrepreneurs, you can navigate your market debut with confidence, setting a strong foundation for sustained growth and success in the digital marketplace.

Mindset for Growth: Cultivating a Positive Outlook and Resilience in the Face of Entrepreneurial Challenges

Embarking on a journey in digital entrepreneurship is synonymous with facing a spectrum of challenges and setbacks. However, these are not roadblocks but rather opportunities for growth and learning. Cultivating a growth mindset is not just beneficial—it's essential for transforming these challenges into valuable lessons and stepping stones toward your success. This section delves into key strategies that will help you develop resilience and maintain a positive outlook, crucial for thriving in the unpredictable terrain of digital entrepreneurship.

Key Concepts and Strategies:

Embrace Challenges as Opportunities: Shift your perspective to see obstacles not as impediments but as invaluable chances to learn, adapt, and innovate. Every challenge you overcome is a testament to your growth and a milestone on your entrepreneurial journey.

Learn from Failures: Embrace a paradigm where failures are not seen as defeats but as rich sources of learning. When things don't go as planned, dissect the experience, extract the lessons, and apply this newfound knowledge to refine your strategies. Remember, every seasoned entrepreneur has a history of learning from their missteps.

Celebrate Small Wins: In the whirlwind of entrepreneurship, it's easy to bypass the small victories. However, recognizing and celebrating these moments is vital for building momentum and staying motivated. These wins are the building blocks of your larger goals.

Continuous Learning: The digital landscape is in a state of constant flux, with new trends and technologies emerging regularly. Commit to lifelong learning to stay relevant and innovative, whether through formal online courses, staying updated with industry publications, or engaging in community forums.

Build a Support Network: Entrepreneurship can be a solitary journey, but you don't have to go it alone. Foster a network of mentors, peers, and supporters who can provide guidance, encouragement, and a fresh perspective when you're navigating tough times.

Maintain Work-Life Balance: It's crucial to find harmony between your entrepreneurial endeavors and personal well-being. Ensure that your drive for success is balanced with activities that rejuvenate and refresh you, safeguarding against burnout.

Visualize Success: Regularly picturing the realization of your goals can be a powerful motivator. Visualization not only keeps you aligned with your objectives but also primes you to tackle challenges with a solution-oriented mindset.

Conclusion

Adopting a growth mindset in the realm of digital entrepreneurship means continuously seeking ways to learn, evolve, and bounce back stronger from setbacks. It's about transforming every experience, good or bad, into a lesson that propels you forward. By embracing this mindset, you'll navigate the entrepreneurial journey with resilience, adaptability, and a constant eye on your long-term vision, laying the groundwork for sustained success and fulfillment.

3

Strategies for Growth and Sustainability

Financial Mastery: Budgeting, Pricing, and Diversification Strategies

In the dynamic realm of digital entrepreneurship, achieving financial mastery is not just beneficial—it's essential for the sustainability and growth of your online business. This section delves into crucial financial strategies, including adept budgeting, astute pricing, and strategic diversification, all aimed at fortifying your venture's financial foundation and fostering growth.

Budgeting for Success

Strategic budgeting goes beyond mere expense tracking; it's about aligning your financial resources with your business's growth objectives:

1. Understanding Cash Flow: Keeping a meticulous record of your income and expenditures is fundamental. Utilize tools like QuickBooks or Excel to gain a clear overview of your financial status and anticipate future cash flow needs.

2. Prioritizing Expenditures: Channel your budget towards activities that drive growth, such as marketing and product development, while keeping unnecessary expenses in check.

3. Preparing for the Unexpected: Establish a contingency fund to navigate unforeseen financial challenges without disrupting your business continuity.

Strategic Pricing

Crafting a pricing strategy is a balancing act between staying competitive and maintaining profitability:

1. Cost-Based Pricing: Calculate the total cost of delivering your product or service and add a markup to ensure profitability.

2. Value-Based Pricing: Set your prices based on the value your customers attribute to your offerings, which might allow for higher price points if the perceived value is substantial.

3. Market Comparison: Regularly assess your pricing in relation to your competitors to ensure you remain attractive to customers without underselling your value.

Diversifying Revenue Streams

Diversification is a key strategy to mitigate risks and stabilize your income:

1. Expand Offerings: Innovate and introduce new products or services that complement and expand your current portfolio.

2. Explore Passive Income: Investigate opportunities like affiliate marketing, digital product creation, or subscription models to establish steady revenue streams.

3. Enter New Markets: Extend your reach to new demographics or geographical areas to tap into new customer bases and revenue opportunities.

Real-Life Application: Sophia Jenkins' Financial Strategy in Action

 Sophia Jenkins' journey from a seasoned professional to a thriving online consultant showcases the impact of strategic financial planning. Her story is more than a list of financial tactics; it's a narrative of how informed decisions can lead to sustainable success in the digital world.

Sophia's financial acumen was evident in her budgeting precision. Using QuickBooks, she didn't just monitor expenses; she forecasted future financial needs, ensuring her business wasn't just surviving, but poised for growth. This wasn't mere number-crunching; it was strategic foresight, allowing her to invest wisely in areas like marketing, which significantly expanded her clientele.

Her approach to pricing was equally thoughtful. Sophia knew her expertise had substantial value. She implemented value-based pricing, not only to reflect her worth but also to attract clients who appreciated her premium service, thereby enhancing her brand's market position.

Diversification was Sophia's key maneuver for financial stability. She didn't settle with her consultancy; she ventured into online courses, tapping into her industry knowledge to reach a broader audience. This move wasn't just about income; it was about building a robust brand presence.

Sophia's success illustrates a balanced approach to financial planning. Her journey demonstrates that strategic budgeting, value-aligned pricing, and income diversification are not just abstract concepts but practical strategies that can forge a path to lasting growth in the digital entrepreneurship landscape.

Conclusion

Mastering the financial aspects of your digital business is not optional—it's critical. Through intelligent budgeting, strategic pricing, and diversification of revenue streams, digital entrepreneurs can secure a firm financial footing, adapt to market fluctuations, and pave the path toward sustained growth and success in the digital marketplace.

Efficiency Through Automation and Outsourcing: Practical Steps to Streamline Operations and Maximize Productivity

In today's fast-paced digital business landscape, efficiency isn't just a goal—it's a necessity for sustainable growth. Leveraging automation and outsourcing can transform your operations, enabling you to focus on the strategic initiatives that truly require your personal touch and expertise.

Automation: Harnessing Your Digital Workforce

Automation is like having an additional team that works tirelessly in the background, handling routine tasks and freeing up your time for high-value activities:

1. Identify Automatable Tasks: Look for repetitive tasks that consume a disproportionate amount of time, such as social media scheduling or email marketing.

2. Select the Right Tools: Choose automation tools that integrate well with your current systems and can scale with your business. Tools should be user-friendly and effective.

3. Implement Gradually: Start with automating one or two processes. Monitor their impact, make necessary adjustments, and expand your use of automation as you become more comfortable.

Outsourcing: Extending Your Team with Expertise

Outsourcing enables you to access specialized skills on demand, enhancing your output quality without the overhead of additional full-time employees:

1. Define Your Needs: Clearly identify the tasks or projects you want to outsource, outlining the skills and experience required.

2. Choose the Right Platforms: Utilize trusted platforms like Upwork or Fiverr to connect with professionals who can bring your projects to life.

3. Communicate Effectively: Provide detailed briefs, establish clear expectations, and maintain open lines of communication to ensure successful collaborations.

Real-Life Application: The Transformation of TechGuru

Anna Rivera (49) and Marco Chen (54), co-founders of TechGuru, recognized that their agency's growth was being hampered by time-consuming operational tasks. Their strategic pivot to automation and outsourcing marked a turning point.

Anna introduced an automated system for client reporting, which reclaimed hours of time each week, enhancing their focus on client engagement and business development. Marco, on the other hand, outsourced content creation, elevating the quality of their output and engaging their audience more effectively.

The result was transformative: TechGuru experienced a 40% boost in productivity and a significant expansion of their client base, illustrating the profound impact of smart automation and strategic outsourcing.

Conclusion

Embracing automation and outsourcing is about working smarter, not harder. These strategies can significantly enhance your operational efficiency, freeing you to focus on the strategic and creative aspects of your business that demand your unique insights. By integrating these approaches, you position your digital business for greater productivity, growth, and long-term success.

Legal Foundations: Essential Legal Considerations for Protecting Your Digital Assets and Intellectual Property

In the ever-evolving digital landscape, safeguarding your intellectual property (IP) and understanding the legal nuances of your online business are not just beneficial—they're imperative for longevity and compliance. This segment offers a primer on the fundamental legal aspects vital for securing your digital assets and ensuring your operation adheres to the law.

Understanding Intellectual Property Rights

Intellectual property rights are the lifeblood of digital businesses, ensuring your creative and innovative outputs are protected:

1. Copyrights: These rights automatically protect your literary and artistic creations, such as articles, blogs, and graphics. Formal registration, while not always necessary, can provide a more substantial legal defense.

2. Trademarks: Registering trademarks for your brand's distinctive elements, like logos and taglines, can significantly enhance your legal protection and aid in brand identity preservation.

3. Patents: If your business involves unique inventions or processes, securing a patent can provide exclusive rights to benefit from your innovation, preventing others from unauthorized usage.

Navigating Online Business Laws

Understanding and complying with online business regulations are crucial for operating legitimately and maintaining consumer trust:

1. Data Protection and Privacy: Familiarize yourself with laws like GDPR or CCPA to ensure you're handling personal data correctly, which is paramount for customer trust and legal compliance.

2. E-commerce Regulations: Be aware of the legalities surrounding digital transactions, advertising, and marketing, which can vary widely across jurisdictions.

3. Terms of Service and Privacy Policies: Craft clear, comprehensive legal documents that outline how you conduct business and manage user data, crucial for transparency and legal protection.

Implementing Protective Measures

Proactive steps toward legal safeguarding fortify your business's security and credibility:

1. Seek Professional Advice: Engaging with legal experts specialized in digital commerce can provide tailored advice and ensure your business is fully safeguarded.

2. Regularly Review Legal Requirements: Stay informed about changes in laws impacting your business and adjust your practices to stay compliant.

3. Educate Your Team: Ensuring your staff understands the legal aspects of their work is essential for maintaining company-wide compliance.

Real-Life Application: CreativeTech's Proactive Legal Strategy

CreativeTech, founded by Julia Martinez (56) and David Lee (55), stands as a paragon of legal diligence in the digital design domain. From inception, they recognized their designs and digital products were invaluable assets needing stringent protection.

Intellectual Property Protection: They didn't merely rely on automatic copyright protections; they proactively registered their trademarks and copyrights, fortifying their legal defense against potential infringements.

Navigating Compliance: Julia and David meticulously adhered to online business laws, especially around data protection, aligning their operations with GDPR to cater to their European clientele confidently.

Drafting Legal Documents: They crafted transparent, user-friendly terms of service and privacy policies, setting clear expectations for their customers and solidifying trust in their brand.

Outcome: These measures didn't just secure CreativeTech's intellectual and digital assets—they enhanced their market reputation, fostering trust and expanding their client base in a competitive industry.

Conclusion

Building a legal framework is foundational for a digital business's security and credibility. By proactively managing your IP rights, staying compliant with online business laws, and ensuring transparency in your operations, you establish a resilient and trustworthy digital enterprise.

Community Engagement: Building and Nurtifying an Online Community to Support and Grow Your Business

In today's digital marketplace, an engaged online community transcends being merely an asset; it acts as a linchpin for fostering brand loyalty, enhancing customer engagement, and driving sustainable growth. A vibrant community not only provides invaluable feedback but also propels your brand through advocacy and direct support.

Understanding the Importance of Community:

A dynamic community serves as a crucial support network, enabling rich interactions between your brand and its audience. This engagement leads to invaluable insights, heightened brand advocacy, and an empowered customer support network, all contributing to your business's resilience and growth.

Strategies for Building Your Community:

1. Platform Selection: Choose a platform that resonates with your audience, whether it's a dedicated forum, social media group, or another interactive space.

2. Value Provision: Consistently deliver content that educates, entertains, and engages your community members.

3. Interaction Encouragement: Foster a participatory environment with discussions, polls, and community highlights.

4. Event Hosting: Virtual events and Q&As can deepen connections and bolster community spirit.

Nurturing Your Community:

Building a community is an ongoing journey:

1. Active Participation: Show your commitment by being actively involved and responsive to community interactions.

2. Member Recognition: Celebrate and highlight contributions to make members feel valued and seen.

3. Adaptive Growth: Evolve with your community, adapting to its changing needs and preferences to maintain engagement.

Real-Life Example: GreenGrowth's Community Dynamics

GreenGrowth, an eco-friendly product startup, harnessed the power of community engagement to amplify their impact. Founders Lisa Nguyen (39)and Raj Patel (51) fostered a digital space where eco-conscious individuals could connect, share, and contribute towards environmental sustainability.

Community Initiation: GreenGrowth's Facebook group quickly became a hub for sharing sustainable practices and discussing eco-innovations, attracting a dedicated following.

Engagement and Interaction: Through regular posts, challenges, and member spotlights, Lisa and Raj cultivated an active and participatory community atmosphere.

Feedback Utilization: The community became a rich source of feedback, directly influencing GreenGrowth's product innovations and driving their brand forward.

Business Impact: This thriving community not only bolstered GreenGrowth's market presence but also created a loyal customer base, demonstrating the tangible benefits of strategic community engagement.

Conclusion:

Effective community engagement is not just about building an audience; it's about fostering a network that actively supports and grows with your business. By nurturing your online community, you lay down a foundation for sustained growth, enhanced brand loyalty, and a resilient business model in the digital age.

4

Navigating the Evolving Digital Landscape

Overcoming Adversity: Identifying Common Obstacles and Strategies to Overcome Them

Embarking on a journey in the digital world is akin to navigating a rapidly shifting terrain where obstacles are part and parcel of the voyage. These hurdles, while daunting, are not insurmountable. They test your resilience, push you to innovate, and ultimately, refine your entrepreneurial acumen. Recognizing these common challenges and arming yourself with effective strategies is pivotal for thriving amidst the digital flux. This segment delves into typical roadblocks digital entrepreneurs face and offers tactical advice for overcoming them, ensuring your journey is marked by growth and perseverance.

Identifying Common Obstacles

1. Technological Changes: The pace at which technology evolves can quickly outdate your methods and tools, necessitating constant adaptation to stay relevant.

2. Market Saturation: With more entities vying for attention in the digital space, differentiating your business becomes increasingly crucial.

3. Cybersecurity Threats: The online nature of digital businesses exposes them to unique vulnerabilities, including the risk of data breaches and cyberattacks.

4. Changing Consumer Behaviors: The digital domain is characterized by rapidly shifting consumer preferences, requiring businesses to be adaptable and responsive.

Strategies to Overcome Obstacles

1. Continuous Learning: Embrace a mindset of perpetual education to keep abreast of new technologies and industry developments, ensuring your business remains resilient and competitive.

2. Differentiation: Establish a clear and compelling unique value proposition (UVP) to set your business apart from competitors, addressing a specific need or niche in a novel way.

3. Robust Security Measures: Prioritize the security of your digital assets and customer information by implementing comprehensive cybersecurity practices and staying updated on best practices to mitigate risks.

4. Customer Engagement: Foster a strong connection with your audience through consistent engagement, listening to their feedback, and adapting your offerings to meet their evolving needs, ensuring your business remains aligned with market demand.

Real-Life Example: Navigating Change at TechAdapt Solutions

TechAdapt Solutions, co-founded by Michael Thompson, 54, and Sandra Lee, 58, exemplifies resilience in the digital sector. Initially a web development firm, they encountered a pivotal challenge as the industry's focus shifted toward mobile and cloud computing, necessitating a strategic transformation to stay relevant.

Identifying the Shift: Michael and Sandra, noticing the industry's evolution, undertook a comprehensive analysis to pinpoint new technological trends and client demands, laying the groundwork for their company's strategic pivot.

Strategic Adaptation: Embracing the industry's move to cloud computing and mobile app development, they invested in upskilling their team and integrating new technologies. This significant shift, though costly, was crucial for staying aligned with the industry's trajectory.

Cybersecurity Enhancement: Transitioning to cloud-based services introduced new cybersecurity imperatives. TechAdapt Solutions responded by fortifying their cybersecurity framework, ensuring robust protection for their and their clients' digital assets.

Deepening Community Ties: Under Sandra's leadership, TechAdapt amplified its engagement with clients, using direct feedback to refine and tailor their offerings. This strategy not only boosted client satisfaction but also provided invaluable insights into the market's evolving needs.

Outcome: This strategic overhaul rejuvenated TechAdapt Solutions, bolstering its market position and attracting a broader client base while maintaining strong relationships with existing customers. Michael and Sandra's proactive approach and commitment to continuous learning and adaptation underscored their success, showcasing the power of resilience and strategic foresight in the digital realm.

Conclusion:

Successfully navigating the digital landscape requires recognizing and overcoming a myriad of challenges, from technological advancements and market saturation to cybersecurity threats and shifting consumer behaviors. By adopting a mindset geared toward continuous learning, differentiation, robust security, and active customer engagement, entrepreneurs can turn potential obstacles into opportunities for growth. The resilience and adaptability demonstrated through strategic planning and community interaction are key to not only surviving but flourishing in the digital realm, setting a solid foundation for sustained business success.

Staying Ahead: Adapting to Market Trends and Technological Advances

In the dynamic realm of digital entrepreneurship, relevance is synonymous with adaptability. The digital landscape doesn't just change; it evolves at breakneck speed, with new technologies and market trends constantly emerging. For entrepreneurs, particularly those venturing into this domain later in life, embracing these changes is crucial— not merely for survival but for flourishing. Here are strategies to ensure your business not only stays competitive but also becomes a beacon of innovation:

Keeping Abreast of Market Trends

1. Continuous Market Research: Stay ahead by constantly monitoring industry trends and shifts in consumer preferences. Utilize resources like Google Trends, social media listening tools, and industry-specific reports to gain a deeper understanding of the market dynamics.

2. Engage with Your Audience: Establish a two-way conversation with your customers. Their feedback is a goldmine of insights, revealing their evolving needs and expectations. Platforms like social media, customer surveys, and interactive feedback sessions can be invaluable in this regard.

3. Network with Peers: Immersing yourself in the community of industry professionals provides a broader perspective on market trends. Engage in industry forums, attend relevant conferences (whether online or face-to-face), and participate in professional networking groups to stay connected and informed.

Leveraging Technological Advances

1. Embrace Innovation: In the digital age, being receptive to new technologies is key to maintaining a competitive edge. Whether it's harnessing AI to offer personalized service or employing blockchain for enhanced transaction security, integrating innovative technologies can significantly elevate your business operations and customer engagement.

2. Invest in Training: To fully leverage these technological advancements, it's crucial that both you and your team are proficient in their use. Engaging in continuous learning through online courses, industry workshops, and webinars can equip you with the necessary skills and knowledge.

3. Partner with Tech Experts: Should the incorporation of new technologies seem daunting, forging partnerships with tech firms or bringing in freelance specialists can be an effective strategy. These experts can facilitate the seamless integration of cutting-edge technologies into your business, ensuring you stay at the forefront of digital innovation.

Agile Product Development

1. Iterative Development: Embracing an agile methodology in product development offers the flexibility to adapt swiftly to market reactions and consumer insights. This approach might involve launching beta versions of your offerings, enabling you to collect valuable feedback early on and make necessary adjustments before a full-scale launch.

2. Customer-Centric Design: The core of your product development should be a deep understanding of your customer's needs and preferences. This involves integrating user feedback, conducting thorough usability tests, and engaging in continuous market research to ensure your products or services resonate with and fulfill the expectations of your target market.

Conclusion

To maintain a competitive edge in the digital domain, it's essential to adopt a forward-thinking approach, keenly attuned to the latest market trends and technological innovations. Staying informed about industry dynamics, wholeheartedly embracing new technologies, and cultivating an agile product development culture are pivotal steps to ensure your venture not only survives but thrives in the digital age. The path of digital entrepreneurship is undeniably one of perpetual evolution and learning. Yet, armed with a strategic approach to adaptation and innovation, this path can unfold into a journey marked by significant growth and enduring success.

Lifelong Learning: The Key to Sustained Success in Digital Entrepreneurship

In the world of digital entrepreneurship, especially for those over 50, education is an endless journey. The digital terrain is perpetually changing, introducing new technologies, evolving consumer preferences, and fresh business strategies. To thrive and maintain relevance in this ever-evolving landscape, a steadfast commitment to lifelong learning is indispensable.

Embracing continuous education and skill development isn't just about staying updated; it's about proactively adapting to change, seizing new opportunities, and consistently refining your approach to business. It involves cultivating a mindset where learning is not seen as a one-time task but as an integral and ongoing part of your entrepreneurial journey.

Whether it's mastering the latest digital marketing tools, understanding emerging e-commerce trends, or exploring new models of customer engagement, the quest for knowledge is what will keep you at the forefront of the digital business world. This commitment to education not only fuels your business's growth but also enriches your personal development, offering a fulfilling path that goes hand in hand with your entrepreneurial aspirations.

Why Continuous Learning Matters

- **Adaptability:** Staying informed about the latest digital trends and technological advancements is not just beneficial—it's essential. It allows entrepreneurs over 50 to remain competitive and responsive to market changes, ensuring their business strategies are aligned with current demands.

- **Innovation:** Lifelong learning is the engine of innovation. It enables entrepreneurs to devise novel solutions and approaches, addressing the dynamic needs of consumers and staying ahead in the digital marketplace.

- **Resilience:** Broadening your knowledge across different aspects of digital entrepreneurship builds resilience. It equips you with the tools to navigate obstacles, recover from challenges, and maintain a forward-moving trajectory despite the ups and downs.

Strategies for Lifelong Learning

- **Online Courses and Webinars:** Platforms like Coursera, Udemy, and LinkedIn Learning offer a wealth of knowledge across various subjects relevant to digital entrepreneurship. These resources provide an opportunity to stay current with industry trends, learn new skills, and deepen your understanding of the digital world.

- **Networking and Community Engagement:** Learning is not just about consuming information; it's also about interaction and collaboration. Engaging with online forums, attending local meetups, or joining professional networks can offer invaluable insights, broaden your perspectives, and provide a sense of community.

- **Experimentation and Practical Application:** Applying what you learn by experimenting and implementing new ideas in real-world settings is crucial. It not only cements your knowledge but also helps you understand the practicality and effectiveness of different strategies and techniques in your own business context.

Real-Life Application: Embracing a New Chapter with Michael Thompson

Michael Thompson, at 63, exemplifies the essence of lifelong learning in the realm of digital entrepreneurship. With a background in engineering and a newly kindled passion for digital marketing, Michael embarked on a transformative journey into a field where he was once a novice.

Eager to master digital marketing, Michael immersed himself in a rigorous self-education regimen. He enrolled in online courses that covered the breadth of digital marketing tactics, actively participated in webinars to stay abreast of the latest industry shifts, and joined digital marketing forums where he exchanged knowledge and insights with peers.

Michael's commitment to learning wasn't confined to virtual classrooms; he put theory into practice by spearheading a digital marketing campaign for a local non-profit organization. This hands-on experience was invaluable, enabling him to hone his skills, experiment with different strategies, and witness the tangible impact of his efforts.

The culmination of Michael's dedication is "Thompson Digital," his consultancy that stands as a testament to the power of continuous learning and adaptation. His services are not only reflective of current digital marketing best practices but are also continually evolving, ensuring that "Thompson Digital" remains at the cutting edge of the industry. Michael's journey is a compelling narrative that illustrates how lifelong learning can pave the way to success and fulfillment in the digital age.

Conclusion

For entrepreneurs over 50 venturing into the digital landscape, lifelong learning is not just beneficial—it's essential. It lays the foundation for adaptability, fuels innovation, and builds resilience, enabling you to navigate the rapid shifts in technology and market dynamics with agility and insight. By committing to continuous learning, you ensure that your digital business not only survives but thrives, staying relevant and dynamic in a constantly changing digital ecosystem. This commitment to education and growth is what keeps your venture at the forefront of innovation, securing its place in the competitive digital marketplace.

5

Beyond Business - A Fulfilling Future

Reflecting on Achievements: Understanding Your Journey and Celebrating Success

Reflection serves as a vital tool for digital entrepreneurs, offering a moment to pause and take stock of the journey traveled. It's an opportunity to not just recount the milestones but to deeply understand the lessons learned, the challenges overcome, and the successes achieved. This practice of looking back is not for mere nostalgia; it's a strategic approach to glean insights from past experiences, fostering a mindset of gratitude and informed perspective that paves the way for future endeavors.

In the fast-paced world of digital entrepreneurship, it's easy to be perpetually forward-looking, chasing the next goal or innovation. However, taking the time to reflect can provide profound benefits. It allows you to acknowledge your growth, appreciate the value of your experiences, and recalibrate your goals with a clearer understanding of what truly matters. This reflective process is essential for continual learning and evolution, ensuring that your future steps are guided by wisdom garnered from the journey thus far.

The Significance of Reflection in Your Entrepreneurial Journey

- **Acknowledgment:** Taking the time to recognize and celebrate your achievements is crucial. It's a way to reinforce your confidence and acknowledge the effort, determination, and resilience that have been integral to your success. This recognition is not just about giving yourself a pat on the back; it's about validating the journey, understanding the importance of each step, and preparing yourself for future challenges with renewed vigor.

- **Gratitude:** Reflection helps cultivate a mindset of gratitude. It allows you to appreciate the people who have supported you, the experiences that have shaped your entrepreneurial spirit, and the opportunities that have spurred your growth. Gratitude enriches your journey, enhancing your overall well-being and fostering positive relationships within your professional network.

- **Learning:** The act of reflecting is a profound learning tool. It enables you to extract lessons from your experiences, both successes and setbacks. This introspection is invaluable for refining your strategies and approaches, ensuring that your future decisions are informed by a comprehensive understanding of what has worked, what hasn't, and why.

Strategies for Effective Reflection in Digital Entrepreneurship

- **Journaling:** Keeping a consistent journal offers a structured way to chronicle your entrepreneurial path. This practice not only captures your achievements and challenges but also serves as a reflective tool, helping you to see patterns, progress, and areas for improvement. It's a space for honest self-assessment and a repository of insights that can guide your future decisions.

- **Milestone Celebrations:** Recognizing and celebrating key milestones is essential for maintaining motivation and perspective. Whether it's a quiet moment of gratitude or a shared celebration with your team or support network, acknowledging these moments reinforces the value of your efforts and the progress you've achieved.

- **Feedback Loops:** Constructive feedback is a cornerstone of growth. Engaging with peers, mentors, or a supportive community can provide you with valuable external perspectives. These interactions can offer encouragement, challenge your thinking, and provide insights that you might not have considered, enriching your reflective practice.

- **Annual Reviews:** Dedicate time each year for an in-depth review of your journey. This annual check-in allows you to evaluate your achievements against your goals, understand the challenges you've faced, and reassess your strategies. It's a strategic pause to realign your objectives and plan for the year ahead, ensuring that your actions are guided by both past lessons and future aspirations.

Leveraging Your Narrative: The Impact of Sharing Your Journey

- **Inspiration:** Your personal and professional saga has the power to inspire others, particularly those who are navigating their own entrepreneurial journeys. By sharing your experiences, the obstacles you've overcome, and the milestones you've reached, you provide a beacon of hope and a practical guide for others. Your story can be the catalyst that encourages someone to take that first leap or to persevere through their challenges.

- **Connection:** When you open up about your journey, you do more than just narrate your achievements; you build deeper connections with your audience. This vulnerability and authenticity add a human element to your brand, making it more relatable and trustworthy. It transforms your audience's perception, allowing them to see the person behind the business and fostering a sense of community and loyalty.

- **Legacy:** Sharing your story does more than chronicle your business's history; it lays the groundwork for your legacy. It's about the impact you leave on individuals and the broader industry, influencing not just current peers and customers but also future entrepreneurs. Your narrative becomes a part of your enduring mark on the world, a testament to your values, your resilience, and your contribution to the field.

Real-Life Example: Charting a New Path with Alex Johnson

At 52, Alex Johnson transitioned from a traditional finance career to establishing an innovative online platform dedicated to financial education. This shift wasn't just a career change; it was a profound learning experience that underscored the importance of reflection in personal and professional growth.

Alex made it a practice to journal diligently, documenting his transition's ups and downs. This habit helped him transform challenges into actionable insights and celebrate achievements as milestones in his entrepreneurial journey. His journal became a treasure trove of experiences, offering clarity, direction, and a sense of accomplishment.

The impact of Alex's journey extended beyond his personal growth and the platform's financial success. By sharing his experiences through blogs and speaking engagements, he offered a narrative that resonated with many, particularly older entrepreneurs who might feel hesitant about the digital world. His story became a source of inspiration, encouraging his peers to embrace technology and innovation, irrespective of their age.

Alex's journey and the way he shared it contributed significantly to building a supportive community around his platform. His reflections, shared openly, encouraged others to embark on their entrepreneurial ventures, fostering a space where age was seen not as a barrier but as an asset. Alex Johnson's story exemplifies how reflecting on and sharing your journey can inspire others, build connections, and create a legacy that influences perceptions and motivates change in the digital entrepreneurship landscape.

Conclusion

Reflection on your achievements transcends mere reminiscence; it is an essential practice that validates your journey, cultivates appreciation, and offers critical insights that guide your path forward. In the realm of digital entrepreneurship, particularly as you navigate this landscape later in life, embracing reflection enables you to acknowledge your progress, celebrate your resilience, and learn from every experience.

As you progress, view each milestone and every hurdle not just as isolated incidents but as formative chapters of your evolving story. This practice isn't just about recording successes or analyzing challenges; it's about recognizing your journey's intrinsic value and how it shapes your entrepreneurial spirit. By valuing reflection, you set the stage for continuous growth, ensuring that your future endeavors are informed by wisdom, gratitude, and a deep understanding of your entrepreneurial narrative.

Mentorship and Legacy: Fostering Growth and
Building a Future

Mentorship plays a pivotal role in digital entrepreneurship,
particularly for those who have garnered wisdom and
experience over the years. It's an opportunity to guide
emerging entrepreneurs, sharing insights and lessons that
can illuminate their paths and accelerate their growth. This
exchange of knowledge is not just an act of giving back but
a means to influence the industry's future positively and
sustainably.

By engaging in mentorship, seasoned entrepreneurs have
the unique opportunity to impart their understanding, help
others navigate the digital landscape, and avoid common
pitfalls. It's a chance to shape the next generation of
entrepreneurs, ensuring they are well-equipped to tackle
the challenges and opportunities that lie ahead.

Moreover, mentorship contributes to the mentor's legacy,
allowing them to leave an indelible mark on the industry
and the individuals they guide. This legacy transcends
business successes, embodying the values, wisdom, and
spirit of innovation that the mentor passes on. It's about
creating a lasting impact that fosters growth, encourages
resilience, and inspires continued innovation in the digital
entrepreneurship realm.

The Ripple Effects of Mentorship

- **For the Mentor:** Engaging in mentorship offers seasoned entrepreneurs a reflective journey, revisiting their own paths while bolstering their knowledge base. It's a gratifying experience that extends beyond personal gain, allowing mentors to invest in the industry's future and witness the tangible impact of their guidance. Mentoring isn't just about teaching; it's a reciprocal process that often provides the mentor with fresh perspectives and renewed motivation.

- **For the Mentee:** Access to a mentor's insights, experiences, and networks can be transformative for emerging entrepreneurs. This relationship provides mentees with a compass to navigate the often-turbulent waters of digital entrepreneurship, offering them a clearer vision and a more strategic approach to their ventures. The mentor's guidance can help mentees sidestep potential pitfalls and fast-track their growth, ultimately leading to more robust and resilient business foundations.

Cultivating a Legacy of Empowerment and Community

Creating a legacy through mentorship is about leaving an imprint that extends far beyond your personal or business achievements. It's about the knowledge shared, the confidence built, and the entrepreneurial spirits kindled. When you dedicate time and energy to support and uplift others, you contribute to a culture where continuous learning, mutual support, and collaborative growth are valued.

This legacy is not just measured by the success of the mentees but also by the broader impact on the digital entrepreneurship ecosystem. It's about fostering an environment where innovation thrives, where diverse voices are heard and respected, and where the next generation feels empowered to explore, create, and lead.

By embedding a legacy of support and education, you ensure that your contributions resonate well into the future, inspiring upcoming entrepreneurs to pursue their visions, overcome obstacles, and, in turn, mentor others. This cyclical process enriches the community, ensuring that the spirit of entrepreneurship continues to evolve and flourish, guided by the wisdom and encouragement of its experienced members.

Strategies for Effective Mentorship

- **Active Listening:** The foundation of impactful mentorship lies in active listening. Take the time to truly understand your mentees' perspectives, challenges, and aspirations. This empathetic approach allows you to provide personalized advice and support, making your mentorship more meaningful and effective.
- **Goal-Oriented Guidance:** Help your mentees establish clear, attainable goals. Work with them to break down these goals into actionable steps, providing a roadmap for success. This structured approach not only gives direction but also empowers mentees to track their progress and celebrate their achievements.

- **Sharing Resources:** As a mentor, you have a wealth of resources at your disposal. Share your knowledge, introduce mentees to your professional network, and guide them to tools and information that can catalyze their growth. This exchange of resources can significantly accelerate a mentee's journey and broaden their perspective.

- **Encouraging Resilience:** Share stories from your own career—especially those that highlight perseverance and overcoming adversity. These narratives can be incredibly motivating for mentees, teaching them to view challenges as opportunities for growth and learning. Your experiences can instill a sense of resilience, encouraging mentees to persist and adapt in the face of obstacles.

Real-Life Example: Maria Gonzales's Impactful Mentorship

Maria Gonzales, at 49, leveraged her extensive background in digital marketing to create a mentorship program specifically designed for women venturing into the tech industry. Through her program, Maria offered personalized guidance, ran educational workshops, and led vibrant discussions on online platforms, focusing on key areas like digital marketing strategies, brand development, and effective professional networking.

Her mentorship went beyond simple advice-giving. Maria created a supportive environment where her mentees could gain confidence, develop their skills, and find their unique voices in the tech world. Her efforts were instrumental in enabling these women to break barriers, secure their places in tech roles, and challenge the industry's gender norms.

The impact of Maria's mentorship extended far beyond the immediate successes of her mentees. It contributed significantly to narrowing the gender gap within the tech community. Moreover, Maria's dedication and success in nurturing new talent in the tech field enhanced her reputation, establishing her as a key advocate for diversity and inclusion in technology. Her work not only changed the lives of the women she mentored but also set a powerful example for others in the industry, showcasing the profound influence that committed mentorship can have on promoting inclusivity and driving change in the tech ecosystem.

Conclusion

Mentorship stands as a mutually enriching bond that not only propels mentees forward but also offers mentors profound insights and fulfillment. It's a dynamic interplay that nurtures growth, sparks innovation, and strengthens the fabric of the digital entrepreneurship community. As you progress in your career, reflecting on how your insights and experiences can uplift emerging talents becomes crucial. Engaging in mentorship allows you to extend your impact within the industry, helping to shape the future while forging a legacy that goes beyond mere business achievements. Embrace the role of a mentor and discover how it can amplify your influence, enrich your professional journey, and contribute to a thriving, supportive ecosystem in digital entrepreneurship.

Embracing a Dynamic Retirement: Integrating Passions, Learning, and Growth

The concept of retirement is evolving, especially in today's digital era. It's no longer just about stepping back from work but rather reimagining your involvement with professional interests, hobbies, and community connections. This period of life offers a unique chance to harmonize passion projects, ongoing education, and self-improvement, crafting a retirement that's as enriching and dynamic as any other phase of your life.

In this new age, retirement opens doors to explore interests with renewed vigor, dive into learning opportunities that were once sidelined, and engage in personal growth that enriches not just yourself but those around you. It's a time to pursue what truly matters to you, transforming these golden years into a vibrant and impactful chapter of your journey."

Reimagining Retirement: Engaging, Exploring, and Enriching Your Life

Engaged Continuity: The digital world is brimming with avenues for maintaining professional activity post-retirement. Whether it's through offering consultancy services, guiding the next generation as a mentor, or venturing into new entrepreneurial landscapes, the digital age allows you to redefine what being 'active' means during retirement.

Exploring Passions: Retirement isn't an end but a new beginning—a chance to immerse yourself in interests that may have taken a backseat during your career. Now is the perfect opportunity to rediscover old hobbies or cultivate new ones, be it in the arts, music, travel, or any other passion that excites you.

Ongoing Learning: The digital era makes it easier than ever to continue your education, regardless of your age. Online platforms provide a plethora of learning opportunities, allowing you to acquire new skills or deepen your expertise in various subjects, keeping you engaged and intellectually sharp.

Contributing to Society: Retirement offers a unique opportunity to give back, leveraging your accumulated knowledge and experience for the greater good. Whether it's through volunteering, mentoring, or starting a social enterprise, your contributions can have a meaningful impact on the community and bring a sense of purpose and satisfaction to your retirement years."

Crafting a Rewarding Retirement: Strategies for Enrichment and Engagement

- **Envisioning Your Future:** Start by defining what a fulfilling retirement looks like for you. Consider how you want to integrate your professional skills, hobbies, and personal development goals. Creating a clear vision will serve as your guidepost, helping you navigate this exciting new chapter with purpose and direction.

- **Financial Strategy:** A worry-free retirement where you can fully embrace your passions requires sound financial planning. This might mean careful budgeting, smart investing, or even finding ways to monetize your hobbies. Ensuring financial stability means you can explore your interests freely, without the shadow of financial concerns.

- **Cultivating Connections:** Retirement is a journey best shared. Building a network of peers, whether through community groups, online forums, or local clubs, can provide valuable camaraderie and support. Engaging with others who have similar interests or are at the same life stage can enhance your retirement experience, offering shared learning and new friendships.

- **Goal Setting:** What milestones do you want to reach in your retirement? Whether it's mastering a new skill, completing a personal project, or achieving a fitness goal, setting clear objectives keeps you engaged and motivated. These goals provide a sense of achievement and progress, making your retirement years not just leisurely but purposeful and fulfilling."

Real-Life Example: John Reynolds's New Chapter

John Reynolds (67), who dedicated over three decades to a successful career as a software engineer, didn't see retirement as the end of his productive years but as an opportunity to embark on a new, fulfilling journey. With a lifelong passion for photography that had taken a backseat to his demanding job, John decided that retirement was the perfect time to pursue this interest more seriously.

Embracing Photography: John's first step was to deepen his understanding of photography. He enrolled in advanced online courses, learning about everything from the technical aspects of camera settings to the art of composition. His commitment to learning paid off, and soon, John was creating stunning photographs that captured the beauty of the natural world and urban landscapes.

Turning Passion into Purpose: John's love for photography quickly evolved into a desire to share his work with others. He established an online gallery where enthusiasts could view and purchase his prints. What started as a hobby turned into a thriving online business, allowing John to connect with fellow photography lovers worldwide.

Giving Back: But John's retirement wasn't just about personal pursuits. He wanted to give back to the community that had supported him throughout his career.

Drawing on his background in technology, John began volunteering at a local community center, teaching coding to underprivileged youth. His classes provided a foundation for these young individuals to pursue careers in tech, combining John's expertise with his passion for mentorship.

Building a Legacy: Through his photography and teaching, John found a sense of purpose that retirement alone couldn't offer. He was not only able to pursue his passion but also to make a meaningful impact on the next generation. John's story became an inspiration to many, showcasing that retirement can be a time of personal growth, community contribution, and the start of exciting new chapters.

Conclusion

In the context of today's digital age, retirement is redefined as a stage of continued growth, exploration, and engagement. It's a time when individuals can leverage their wealth of experience while embracing new opportunities for personal and professional development. By thoughtfully planning this phase, individuals can ensure their retirement is marked not by a winding down, but by an invigorating journey of discovery, fulfillment, and meaningful contributions. Whether through pursuing passions, engaging in lifelong learning, or giving back to the community, a well-designed retirement can be a rich, rewarding, and dynamic extension of one's life narrative.

Conclusion: Embarking on Your Digital Adventure

Thank you for exploring "The 50+ Freedom Formula: Redefining Retirement" as you embark on or enhance your journey in digital entrepreneurship. Together, we've delved into the essentials of initiating a digital business, tackled common challenges, and highlighted the significance of technology, community, and continuous learning. Now, it's time to put these insights into practice.

A Call to Action:

Embark on your digital entrepreneurship journey with determination and inquisitiveness. Use this book as your blueprint, but remember, the essence of transformation lies in taking action. Here are some immediate steps to get started:

1. Register a Domain: Secure an online home for your business. Choose a name that reflects your brand and register it.

2. Outline Your Business Plan: Draft a simple plan that outlines your goals, target audience, and how you intend to reach them.

3. Join Online Communities: Connect with like-minded individuals by joining digital entrepreneurship forums or groups in your field.

The Path Forward:

The digital world is ever-evolving, inviting you to grow and adapt continually. Stay inquisitive, embrace lifelong learning, and remain agile to navigate the shifting sands of digital entrepreneurship. Approach each hurdle as an opportunity to learn and expand your horizons.

Leveraging This Book's Insights:

As you progress, draw upon the strategies and stories shared in this book. Combine them with the wisdom of your peers and the support of online communities. Digital entrepreneurship is a shared expedition, enriched by collective wisdom and collaborative effort.

Realizing Your Digital Empire:

Visualize your digital business not just as a goal but as an unfolding reality shaped by your actions. Infuse your venture with your values and the unique perspective you bring. Let this conclusion be not an end, but a beacon guiding you toward a future filled with achievement, creativity, and fulfillment. The journey is ongoing, and it's yours to embrace and enjoy.

Afterword: Igniting Your Path Forward

As you conclude "The 50+ Freedom Formula: Redefining Retirement," my aspiration is that you're imbued with a renewed sense of purpose, armed with actionable insights to embark on or enhance your digital entrepreneurship journey. This guide was conceived not merely to impart knowledge but to spark an awakening within you—an acknowledgment that the digital world is ripe with opportunities for those who are bold, persistent, and open to embracing new beginnings, regardless of age.

Reflecting upon the diverse tales of resilience, creativity, and success that underpin this narrative, it's evident that our shared story is one of unyielding pursuit—chasing fulfillment, independence, and the joy of bringing our passions to life. Your decision to step into the realm of digital entrepreneurship marks a courageous leap towards redefining your narrative, challenging age-old stereotypes, and crafting a legacy that transcends conventional retirement.

This guide's aim was to be your digital compass, illuminating the path from aspiration to actualization. However, the real adventure lies ahead, propelled by the insights you've garnered and the choices you'll make.

As you forge ahead, bear in mind that the strategies and lessons encapsulated in these pages are not static. They are meant to evolve as you grow and as the digital landscape transforms. Stay inquisitive, commit to continuous learning, and be prepared to pivot, adapting to the incessant shifts in technology and market dynamics.

I encourage you to take proactive steps toward realizing your digital aspirations. Whether that's initiating a blog to document your entrepreneurial voyage, engaging in online learning to sharpen your digital skills, or connecting with fellow trailblazers in online or local entrepreneur communities—every action propels you closer to your goals.

A Word of Appreciation and Inspiration

Crafting this book has been a journey of introspection and celebration—pondering the transformative power of digital entrepreneurship and honoring the extraordinary individuals who venture along this path. Thank you for allowing me to be part of your expedition. Your resolve to redefine the traditional contours of retirement and pursue a path laden with learning, innovation, and fulfillment is genuinely inspiring.

Consider John's narrative, a narrative that resonates with many: transitioning from a career in software engineering to embracing a passion for photography, learning new skills, sharing his insights, and giving back to his community. His story exemplifies how retirement can be a stage of exploration, contribution, and profound satisfaction.

Embark on Your Next Chapter

Let the end of this book not signify a conclusion but a catalyst for your ongoing odyssey. The digital expanse is vast, filled with untold success stories and opportunities for innovation and growth, awaiting your unique contribution. Embark on this journey, craft your story, establish your digital presence, and redefine the essence of your coming years.

Here's to your continued journey, a journey where your digital entrepreneurship dreams become a vivid and rewarding reality.

With warm regards,

G. Scott

Disclaimer

The information provided in "The 50+ Freedom Formula: Redefining Retirement" is for general informational and educational purposes only. The author and publisher have made every effort to ensure that the information provided in this book was accurate at the time of publication, but neither the author nor the publisher assumes any responsibility for errors, omissions, or contrary interpretation of the subject matter herein.

This book does not constitute financial, legal, or professional advice. The reader should consult with a professional where appropriate. The author and publisher do not warrant the performance, effectiveness, or applicability of any sites listed or linked to in this book.

All links are for information purposes only and are not warranted for content, accuracy, or any other implied or explicit purpose. The case studies and examples provided within are for illustrative purposes and should not be considered as guarantees of success. Individual results may vary and depend on many factors including individual effort, experience, and circumstances.

No guarantee is made that the reader will achieve results similar to those described in the book. The strategies, tips, and tools mentioned in the book are provided as suggestions and should be evaluated and adapted to the reader's personal situation.

The views and opinions expressed are those of the author and do not necessarily reflect the official policy or position of any associated agency or government body. Names, characters, businesses, places, events, and incidents are